# Contents

Some words are printed in bold, **like this**. You can find out what they mean in the glossary.

## Why Science Matters

# Predicting Earthquakes

**John Farndon**

Heinemann
**LIBRARY**

**www.heinemannlibrary.co.uk**
Visit our website to find out more information about **Heinemann Library** books.

To order:
☎ Phone 44 (0) 1865 888066
▤ Send a fax to 44 (0) 1865 314091
▣ Visit the Heinemann Bookshop at www.heinemannlibrary.co.uk to browse our catalogue and order online.

Heinemann Library is an imprint of Capstone Global Library Limited, a company incorporated in England and Wales having its registered office at 7 Pilgrim Street, London, EC4V 6LB – Registered company number: 6695582

Heinemann is a registered trademark of Pearson Education Limited, under licence to Capstone Global Library Limited

Text © Capstone Global Library Limited 2009
First published in hardback in 2009
Paperback edition first published in 2010

Editorial: Andrew Farrow, Megan Cotugno, and Harriet Milles
Design: Steven Mead and Q2A Creative Solutions
Illustrations: Gordon Hurden
Picture research: Ruth Blair
Production: Alison Parsons

Originated by Modern Age Repro House Ltd
Printed and bound in China by Leo Paper Products Ltd

ISBN: 978 0 4310 4056 1 (hardback)
13 12 11 10 09
10 9 8 7 6 5 4 3 2 1

ISBN: 978 0 4310 4063 9 (paperback)
14 13 12 11 10
10 9 8 7 6 5 4 3 2 1

**British Library Cataloguing-in-Publication data**
Farndon, John
Predicting earthquakes. - (Why science matters)
551.2'2
A full catalogue record for this book is available from the British Library.

**Acknowledgements**
The publisher would like to thank the following for permission to reproduce photographs: © CNES/E. Grimault, 2003 p. **30**; © Corbis pp. **4**, **41** (Pallava Bagla), **7** (Lloyd Cluff), **22** (Roger Ressmeyer), **25** (Jim Sugar), **29**, **31**, **35** (Danny Lehman), **37** (Phil Schermeister); © Corbis/ABC Basin Ajansi/Sygma p. **27**; © Corbis/Bettman p. **26**; © Corbis/Courtesy of Twentieth Century Fox/Bureau L.A. Collection p. **47**; © Corbis/Issei Kato/Reuters p. **36**; © Corbis/Reuters p. **14**; © Getty Images/AFP Photo/Jiji Press p. **45**; © Getty Images/AFP Photo/Raveendran p. **23**; © Getty Images/Yoshikazu Tsuno/AFP p. **38**; © PA Photos/AP Photo/Eric Skitzi p. **43**; © Science Photo Library pp. **13** (US Department of Energy), **15**; © UC Davis Computational Science and Engineering Center p. **34**; © University of California, Berkley/Karl V. Steinbrugge Collection, Earthquake Engineering Research Center pp. **24**, **32**; © U.S. Geological Survey Photographic Library p. **33**. Background images supplied by © istockphoto.

Cover photograph of construction workers trying to assess the damage to an expressway in Kobe, Japan after an earthquake in 1995, reproduced wth permission of © Corbis/TWPhoto and © istockphoto.

The publishers would like to thank Andrew Solway for his invaluable assistance in the preparation of this book.

Every effort has been made to contact copyright holders of any material reproduced in this book. Any omissions will be rectified in subsequent printings if notice is given to the publishers.

# Earthquake probe

Many of the world's major cities, such as Los Angeles, Mexico City, and Tokyo, are sitting on a time bomb. They are located in areas prone to earthquakes. People in places like these learn to live with frequent minor shakings of the ground, called tremors. Yet, sooner or later, one of these cities is likely to be hit by a "Big One" – a devastating earthquake that could claim thousands of lives and destroy vast areas of a city in just a few moments. A big earthquake could be just as dangerous for people in remote areas, far from emergency help.

As yet, we cannot predict where earthquakes will happen. For **seismologists** (earthquake experts), it is a race against time to find a way of predicting earthquakes. This way they might at least provide some warning for people. As this book shows, future breakthroughs in earthquake science might find a way to save countless lives.

A large building in Kobe, Japan topples over after enduring the wrath of the Kobe earthquake.

Almost every day there is an earthquake somewhere in the world. Most are so faint they couldn't even spill a glass of water, and can only be detected by the most sensitive equipment. Fortunately, only a few are big enough to cause devastation. All kinds of things can trigger an earthquake, from a landslide or a volcanic eruption to a heavy truck rumbling by, and an earthquake can occur almost anywhere. However, nearly all major earthquakes are caused by powerful movements deep within the Earth's rocky shell or **crust**.

**CASE STUDY**

## Mallet's quake map

Irish engineer Robert Mallet (1810–1881) was the first great pioneer of earthquake study. He was fascinated by earthquakes and in the 1840s spent long hours setting off explosions in the ground to study how the shock waves moved away from the blast. In particular, he discovered that shock waves move differently through sand and through solid rock.

In 1857, after a bad earthquake in southern Italy, Mallet was determined to go there and see for himself the effects of a real earthquake. He persuaded London's Royal Society to give him a grant and he went to Italy. His first step was to plot exactly where the damage had occurred. Looking at the extent of cracks in houses, he realized there was a central point where shaking was most severe. Away from this point, which scientists later called the **epicentre**, the shaking – and the damage it caused – got less and less.

Over 20 years, he plotted the epicentres of known earthquakes in the past to create an earthquake map of the world. The map revealed that major earthquakes don't just occur anywhere, but cluster in particular regions, later called **earthquake zones**. Mallet had no idea why this might be so, but for the first time people knew where earthquakes are likely to occur.

# Earthquakes and plates

The vast majority of earthquakes occur in certain belts or earthquake zones. Indeed, 80 percent of all big quakes strike around the edge of the Pacific Ocean.

For a long while, no-one knew why. Then in the 1960s, scientists discovered that the Earth's crust is broken into around 20 gigantic floating rafts known as plates. The plates float on the hot, partly melted rock of the **mantle**, the Earth's deep interior beneath the surface. Ferocious heat bubbling up from the centre of the Earth keeps the mantle churning like boiling porridge. As the mantle churns, it keeps the plates constantly drifting on top, moving just a few centimetres each year.

Very soon, scientists realized that most earthquake zones occur along **plate boundaries**. However, not all earthquakes happen on boundaries. For example, in 1811–1812, a huge quake rocked Missouri in the United States, far from any boundaries. In 1992, another struck the Dutch-Belgian-German border, again far from any boundary. Scientists are still puzzled about why this happened.

The concentration of earthquakes around the Pacific Ocean matches the edges of the giant plate under the Pacific Ocean. Scientists believe that the movement of tectonic plates sets off earthquakes.

NORTH AMERICAN

NORTH AMERICAN

EURASIAN

JUAN DE FUCA

CARIBBEAN

ARABIAN

PHILIPPINE

PACIFIC

INDIAN

AFRICAN

COCOS

PACIFIC

NAZCA

SOUTH AMERICAN

AUSTRALIAN

SCOTIA

ANTARCTIC

## THE SCIENCE YOU LEARN: CONTINENTAL DRIFT

In the 1920s, German scientist Alfred Wegener (1880–1930) came across an article showing that many fossils from Africa were strangely similar to fossils in South America. After some research, Wegener came up with a bold explanation. The fossils were similar because, long ago, the continents had been part of a single, giant supercontinent. Other scientists thought Wegener's ideas about **continental drift** were ridiculous, but now we know he was right.

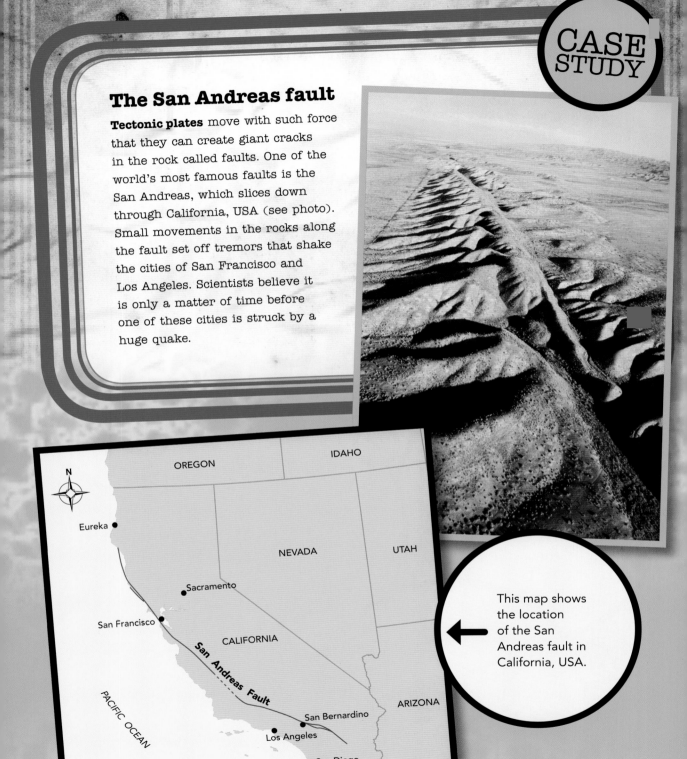

## The San Andreas fault

**Tectonic plates** move with such force that they can create giant cracks in the rock called faults. One of the world's most famous faults is the San Andreas, which slices down through California, USA (see photo). Small movements in the rocks along the fault set off tremors that shake the cities of San Francisco and Los Angeles. Scientists believe it is only a matter of time before one of these cities is struck by a huge quake.

OREGON

IDAHO

Eureka

NEVADA

UTAH

Sacramento

San Francisco

CALIFORNIA

San Andreas Fault

PACIFIC OCEAN

San Bernardino

ARIZONA

Los Angeles

San Diego

MEXICO

0   100 miles

0   100 kilometres

This map shows the location of the San Andreas fault in California, USA.

## Starting a quake

Scientists believe most earthquakes are triggered by plates sliding past each other. The plates don't always slide past each other easily. Instead, there is friction as they rub roughly together. If the friction is low, the rocks can creep past each other with little effect. This is called **fault creep**.

If the friction is high, the rocks may jam together. For a while, the rocks either side of the fault will bend or even stretch a little as they strain past each other. Sooner or later, the rocks suddenly break altogether, sending shock waves through the ground and causing an earthquake. Scientists call this elastic rebound. This is because the rocks first bend and stretch like elastic, then suddenly rebound as they crack. The rupture spreads along the fault boundary like a crack spreading through glass. The longer the crack, the bigger the quake.

fault line

shock waves

In the elastic rebound theory, quakes start along sliding faults between tectonic plates (1). As the plates scrape against one another, stress builds up (2). The rocks become more and more distorted. The bent edges of rock snap straight again, sending out shock waves (3). The fault slips (4).

An earthquake's shock waves travel at different speeds through different materials, and change direction as they pass into denser materials. This is similar to the way light is refracted (bent) as it passes through glass. By timing how long waves take to reach different places, scientists can work out whether the waves have travelled directly there, or have been bent by passing through denser material. Using such methods, they have worked out a huge amount of detail about the Earth's interior.

Most scientists think elastic rebound only partly explains how earthquakes start. Rocks along a fault should get warm with all the friction between them. Yet this doesn't seem to happen. Measurements also show that the rocks are less stressed than expected.

Increasingly, scientists are looking at how fluids oozing between the rocks could lubricate (oil) the fault and reduce friction. Fluids might have become trapped in the fault when it was formed, for instance. Or water could have seeped into the cracks. However, fluids could have opposite effects. In some cases, fluids may make earthquakes less likely by allowing the sides of the fault to slip past each other more easily. Fluids can also make earthquakes *more* likely by encouraging the rocks to slip when they were previously stuck together.

## IN YOUR HOME: FRICTION AND LUBRICATION

When two things rub past each other, they act as a brake on each other. Each surface tries to stop the other sliding past. This braking force is called friction. The rougher the two surfaces, the greater the friction, and the greater the force needed to overcome it. Friction is reduced if the two surfaces are kept apart by a thin film of oil or other liquid. This stops any rough parts of the surfaces from snagging on each other. This is called lubrication. Skates slide easily on ice because the pressure of the blade melts the ice, creating a thin film of lubricating water under the skate.

## The heart of a quake

The place where an earthquake starts is called its origin. Often the earthquake begins with movement over a large area, but there is usually one point where it is at its most intense. This is called the earthquake **focus**, or **hypocentre**. It is from here that shock waves shudder out in all directions. The shock waves are at their most powerful at the focus, and become gradually weaker further away. Most earthquakes start underground. Their effects on the surface are most intense directly above the hypocentre. This point is the epicentre.

The majority of earthquakes are described as shallow-focus, because they begin less than 60 km (37 miles) underground. Shallow-focus quakes are often very powerful. Because rocks near the surface are quite rigid, a lot of stress can build up before they finally break. Shallow earthquakes make their effects felt powerfully on the surface, and cause the most devastation. Most Californian quakes are especially shallow, starting less than 10 km (6 miles) down.

The most surface damage in an earthquake happens in the area above the focus, or hypocentre, called the epicentre.

Fault

Epicentre

Hypocentre

## THE SCIENCE YOU LEARN: PINPOINTING EARTHQUAKE EPICENTRES

Pinpointing a quake's origin is not easy. Earthquake monitoring devices called seismographs (see page 14) can only give a rough idea of the direction a quake is coming from. However, scientists can work out how far away it is from the time lag between the first earthquake waves and the **secondary waves** (see page 12). They draw a circle on a map at this distance around the monitoring station. Then they draw similar circles for the quake's distance from at least three other monitoring stations. The epicentre of the quake is the point where these circles overlap.

Along the deep ocean trenches to the east of Japan, quakes are shallow-focus. Yet, towards the Asian mainland, earthquakes start deeper and deeper. Below the Japanese Islands quakes start at depths of 80–240 km (50–150 miles), at 480 km (300 miles) beneath the Sea of Japan, and at 640 km (400 miles) down under Manchuria on the coast of China. These deeper quakes occur because the Pacific tectonic plate is being subducted (dragged beneath) the Asian plate. The deeper the plate is subducted, the deeper the quakes begin.

A subduction zone is where one plate is forced down beneath another. Where it first shudders downwards, it sets off shallow earthquakes as it rubs against the top plate. As it plunges deeper, the pressures set off deeper quakes.

Deep ocean trench

Continental plate

Oceanic plate

SUBDUCTION ZONE

Plate melts to create volcano

Shallow earthquakes

Deep-focus earthquakes

## Seismic waves

It is impossible to run away from an earthquake. The **seismic waves** (shock waves) move incredibly fast. The fastest waves move through the ground at 5 km (3 miles) per second – 20 times the speed of sound. Even the slowest move through solid rock too fast for the eye to see.

The diagram shows the different types of seismic waves: a) P waves; b) Rayleigh waves; c) S waves; d) Love waves.

a) P wave

b) Rayleigh wave

There are several different types of wave. **Body waves** move through the ground from the underground hypocentre. The fastest body waves are called **primary (P) waves**. These are felt first in an earthquake. P waves move through the ground by compressing and then stretching the rocks. They are also called **compressional waves**. Because P waves compress air as well as rocks, they create a loud roar. **Secondary (S) waves** are slightly slower and snake from side to side. They are also called **shear waves**.

When body waves reach the surface, they are transformed into **surface waves**. P waves become **Rayleigh waves**, which move the ground up and down like waves in the sea. S waves become **Love waves**, which shake the ground from side to side. Surface waves are slower than body waves, but they do most of the damage in an earthquake.

c) S wave

d) Love wave

### CUTTING EDGE: SOUNDING THE ALARM

S waves do the damage in an earthquake, but P waves travel much faster and arrive first. A network of monitoring stations to detect the P waves from an approaching quake could send out an alarm. Such a system is already in widespread use in Japan. The warning is instantly broadcast on television and radio, and alarms sound in schools and factories. Similar systems are working in Mexico, Taiwan, and Turkey, and are being developed in the United States.

Just like a big bell hit by a hammer, the Earth rings for days or even weeks after a big earthquake. Earth's ringtone is far too deep for us to hear. Humans can hear deep bass notes that vibrate about 20 times a second. Some moths can hear sounds that vibrate once every 10 seconds. The Earth's sound vibrates about once every 50 minutes as it rings! It makes the ground rise and fall by about 1 cm (0.4 in) each time – too little for us to notice, but enough to be detected on sensitive scientific equipment.

CASE STUDY

## Detecting secret nuclear tests

Just like earthquakes, big underground explosions send shock waves through the ground. Seismographs can detect these shock waves (see page 14). The seismic waves from explosions create slightly different patterns on the **seismogram** from those generated by earthquakes. During the Cold War (mid-1940s to late 1980s), spies used seismographs to detect whether their rivals were conducting secret tests of nuclear weapons.

Today, more than 170 of the world's nations have signed an agreement called the Comprehensive Test Ban Treaty (CTBT) to ban the testing of nuclear weapons. An important part of the treaty is to make sure no-one is cheating. A network of over 300 seismogram stations is being set up around the world to detect large underground explosions.

The photo shows an underground nuclear testing site in the state of Nevada, USA. The depressions in the earth have been caused by huge underground explosions.

# Quake Watch

Scientists use a seismograph to measure exactly how big a quake is, and to detect all the less obvious earth tremors.

The principle behind a seismograph is simple. If you dangle a weight, such as a ball, on a string then jerk your hand sideways, you will find the ball pauses for a moment before following your hand movement. This slight time lag (delay) is caused by the ball's inertia, or reluctance to move.

Most seismographs contain such dangling weights, or pendulums. When an earthquake shakes the ground, it shakes the whole frame of the seismograph first, but the pendulum stays still for a moment before it starts to swing. The more powerful the earthquake, the more the frame shakes, and the further it moves before the pendulum starts to swing. It is this slight difference in movement that the seismograph records. The movement is converted into an electrical signal and recorded either on magnetic tape or computer.

A seismologist at Taiwan's Central Weather Bureau in Taipei, points out the reading for an earthquake measuring 6.2 on the **Richter scale** on a seismograph.

## Shaking the dragon

The first seismograph was made almost 1,900 years ago in China. It was invented by the philosopher Zhang Heng (AD 78–139), and was called the Didong, or dragon jar. It was a jar with a pendulum hanging under the lid. Eight dragon heads were arranged around the rim of the jar. When a tremor shook the ground, the pendulum swung and tripped the lever on one of the dragon heads. The dragon then dropped a ball into the mouth of one of the frogs arranged around the bottom of the jar. A ball in the mouth of a frog showed that an earthquake had happened and in which direction.

On a seismograph, dangling pendulums swing from side to side to record horizontal shaking (S waves and Love waves). Pendulums that bob up and down on a spring record vertical shaking (P waves and Rayleigh waves).

Pendulum

## CUTTING EDGE: 3D EARTHQUAKE MODELLING

The Quake Project at the Southern California Earthquake Center, USA, is using a supercomputer and very detailed seismograph data to build a 3D computer model of what happens in the ground during an earthquake. They then run events back through time to simulate exactly how the quake developed. By running the clock backwards, scientists can work out the rock structure of the area from its effects on earthquake waves. They can also begin to create computer models that will help predict how earthquakes develop.

## How big is a quake?

News reports usually describe earthquake size in terms of the Richter scale. This scale was devised in 1935 by Californian seismologist Charles Richter (1900–1983). It is an estimate of how strong the seismic waves were right at the focus of the earthquake. Seismologists get this figure using readings from a seismograph at a known distance from the epicentre, or, more accurately, by comparing readings from several seismographs.

The Richter scale rates earthquakes according to the **magnitude** (size) of the strongest waves recorded on the seismograph. The tiniest detectable tremor rates at just above zero, and the biggest quakes ever recorded rate greater than nine. The scale is divided into two parts. Smaller quakes that are felt strongly only close to the focus are rated by their body waves on a scale called the body-wave magnitude (Mb) scale. This works for quakes up to about 6.5 in strength. Body waves from a big quake felt far away all appear to be the same size, so big quakes are rated by surface waves, on the surface-wave magnitude (Ms) scale. The Ms scale works for quakes between 6.5 and 8.0.

Not even the Ms scale works well for the very biggest quakes. In 1977, Japanese seismologist Hiroo Kanamori devised the **moment magnitude (Mw)** scale. This scale uses the seismic moment to work out the energy released in a quake. The seismic moment is a measure of how far and how strongly the rock is moved. It's a complex calculation, but seismologists can use it to come up with a figure that works for tiny and huge quakes. Most big earthquakes up to 9.5 are now measured on this scale.

## CUTTING EDGE: DRILLING FOR QUAKES

Most earthquake monitoring stations are on the Earth's surface, but in California's San Andreas Fault Observatory at Depth (SAFOD) scientists are drilling down into the Earth. They have drilled 3 km (1.9 miles) into an active fault to look at where a quake begins deep underground. "It's like we've been gazing at this game from a distance for decades," says SAFOD project director Bill Ellsworth. "Now someone has given us front row seats. Our noses will be pushed up against the glass, at the heart of the action." With SAFOD, scientists will be able to observe not just the movement of the rocks, but analyse the chemical changes, too.

# CUTTING EDGE: GLOBAL QUAKE WATCH

Seismographic stations are being linked together to keep an eye on earthquake activity around the world. The Global Seismographic Network (GSN) keeps 138 stations linked via the Internet to quickly detect and pinpoint every significant earthquake. The Sumatran earthquake on 26 December 2004 was the first real test for the GSN. It built a detailed picture of the quake within minutes of the first vibration and allowed scientists to understand more about the internal structure of the Earth.

This map shows the world's seismographic stations.

NORTH AMERICA

EUROPE

ASIA

AFRICA

SOUTH AMERICA

AUSTRALASIA

ARCTIC

ANTARCTICA

ANTARCTICA

● Global Seismographic Stations

0          2000 miles

0      2000 kilometres
Scale at the Equator

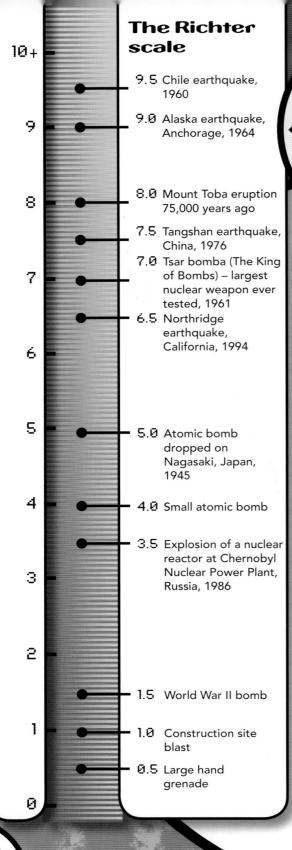

## The Richter scale

9.5   Chile earthquake, 1960

9.0   Alaska earthquake, Anchorage, 1964

8.0   Mount Toba eruption 75,000 years ago

7.5   Tangshan earthquake, China, 1976

7.0   Tsar bomba (The King of Bombs) – largest nuclear weapon ever tested, 1961

6.5   Northridge earthquake, California, 1994

5.0   Atomic bomb dropped on Nagasaki, Japan, 1945

4.0   Small atomic bomb

3.5   Explosion of a nuclear reactor at Chernobyl Nuclear Power Plant, Russia, 1986

1.5   World War II bomb

1.0   Construction site blast

0.5   Large hand grenade

This diagram shows some world events and their measurements on the Richter Scale. 9.5 is the highest recorded measurement to date. However, the scale has no upper limit.

## Earthquake intensity

Seismographs and the Richter scale give an accurate measurement of how powerful an earthquake is, but no idea of its effect. A magnitude 8.5 earthquake in the middle of nowhere will do little damage, while a magnitude 5.0 right under a big city could be devastating. The **Mercalli scale** is sometimes used to measure an earthquake's **intensity** – its visible effects on the ground. The Mercalli scale was devised in 1902 by Italian earthquake scientist Giuseppe Mercalli (1850–1914). It was modified in the 1930s, which is why the version used today is called the Modified Mercalli scale.

It is not a very scientific scale because it depends entirely on human assessments of the damage done. However, it is a useful way to compare different earthquakes and to estimate the strength of earthquakes in historic times, before the invention of the seismograph.

Some of the damage descriptions on the Mercalli scale work all around the world, such as whether the quake is felt only by people lying down. Other descriptions, such as damage to buildings, depend on how well the houses are built.

# The Modified Mercalli scale

**I** — Tremor so faint it is usually only detectable with a seismograph.

**II** — Shaking that can only be felt by someone lying on the floor, especially on upper floors of buildings.

**III** — Shaking felt quite noticeably indoors, especially on upper floors. It can often feel similar to a truck rumbling past.

**IV** — Felt by a few indoors during the day time, but no-one outdoors. At night, sleepers might wake up. Dishes, windows, and doors rattle. Walls may make a cracking sound. It may feel as though a heavy truck has hit the building. Stationary cars may visibly rock.

**V** — Felt by nearly all. Sleepers wake. Dishes, windows, and doors may break. Vases and bottles may tip over. Trees and poles may begin to tilt. Pendulum clocks stop.

**VI** — Felt by all. Generally frightening. Heavy tables and chairs shift. Plaster may fall from the ceiling. Chimneys may topple. Otherwise, only slight damage.

**VII** — A serious quake. Only slight damage in strongly constructed buildings, but can be considerable in poorly built or badly designed buildings. Hard to stand upright. Felt by car drivers.

**VIII** — The strongest buildings survive intact, but there may be considerable damage to ordinary substantial buildings. Poorly built buildings may be completely destroyed. Chimneys, factory stacks, and statues may topple.

**IX** — Even strong buildings may be badly damaged. Major buildings may collapse. Underground pipes may be broken.

**X** — Most buildings are badly damaged or even destroyed. The ground is cracked and rails are bent. Landslides frequent.

**XI** — Devastating, with few buildings left standing. Bridges collapse. Giant cracks open in the ground. Underground pipes are wrecked. Rails are twisted badly.

**XII** — Total destruction. All buildings are destroyed. Cities are laid flat. The ground is badly distorted. Objects are thrown in the air.

# INVESTIGATION: BUILD YOUR OWN SEISMOGRAPH

Professional seismographs are extremely sophisticated, sensitive pieces of equipment. Nevertheless, it is possible to build a simple version that will detect even quite small tremors. The seismograph will give a reading that gives an indication of the magnitude of vibrations in the ground. The vibrations may come from an earthquake, or from someone jumping up and down near the seismograph. It is best to locate the seismograph as far as possible from busy roads because the heavy traffic will affect the instrument. In some places, it might even be able to detect an underground train approaching. With a seismograph like this, you can keep a complete record of earthquake activity in your local region.

Compare your results with those recorded by the Global Seismic Monitor at www.iris.edu/seismon/. This site shows all the quakes above magnitude 4 recorded in the last five years. You can also see up-to-date seismogram readings for many places in the United States, UK, Japan, and New Zealand by following the links from http://earthquake.usgs.gov/eqcenter/helicorders.php

## Equipment:

- wooden base 25 × 60 × 1 cm (10 × 24 × 0.5 in)
- wooden stand 5 × 10 × 5 cm (2 × 4 × 12 in)
- two wooden support blocks 5 × 10 × 20 cm (2 in × 4 in × 8 in)
- wooden beam 2.5 × 2.5 × 50 cm (1 × 1 × 20 in)
- two lengths of wooden dowel, diameter 0.5 cm (0.25 in), length 25 cm (10 in), slender enough to slide through the centre of adding machine paper roll, brick, or other compact, heavy weight
- strong wire, or non-elastic thick rope or twine 2 m (6.5 ft) long
- roll of adding machine paper, width should be greater than or equal to 5 cm (2 in)
- smooth-sided can with lid and base (similar dimensions to paper roll)
- round-headed screw, bolt, or nail 2.5 cm (1 in) long
- soft lead pencil
- nails of various sizes
- masking tape, strapping tape, or duct tape

NOTE: Ask an adult to help you with the drilling part of the assembly.

If you are ambitious, you could fix up a motor from a toy construction to drive round the dowel smoothly, perhaps using a rubber wheel as a contact. Otherwise you will have to move the roller round gradually by hand.

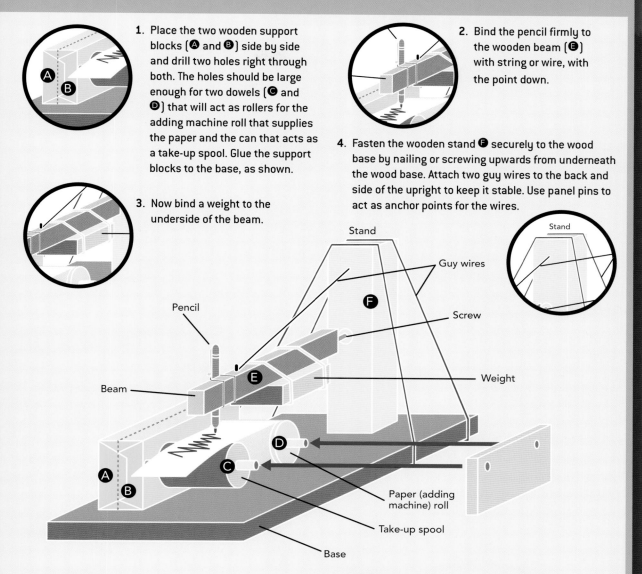

1. Place the two wooden support blocks (Ⓐ and Ⓑ) side by side and drill two holes right through both. The holes should be large enough for two dowels (Ⓒ and Ⓓ) that will act as rollers for the adding machine roll that supplies the paper and the can that acts as a take-up spool. Glue the support blocks to the base, as shown.

2. Bind the pencil firmly to the wooden beam (Ⓔ) with string or wire, with the point down.

4. Fasten the wooden stand Ⓕ securely to the wood base by nailing or screwing upwards from underneath the wood base. Attach two guy wires to the back and side of the upright to keep it stable. Use panel pins to act as anchor points for the wires.

3. Now bind a weight to the underside of the beam.

Stand

Guy wires

Pencil

Screw

Weight

Beam

Paper (adding machine) roll

Take-up spool

Base

5. Insert a screw into one end of the wood beam. This will rest against the upright. Drill a tiny pit for it in the upright. Suspend the middle of the beam with a wire from the upright so that it hangs level.

6. Set up the support blocks on the base. Insert the two dowels through the blocks and the adding machine roll and can, making sure both can rotate freely. Tape down the end of the paper roll onto the can so that when you rotate the dowel holding the can, the paper should wind around the can.

# The effects of a quake

The most dramatic and obvious effect of an earthquake is the shaking ground. Objects on the surface move rapidly to and fro. They only move short distances but with unimaginable power. Some tremors shake the objects from side to side; some lift them a little way, then let them drop. The severity of the shaking depends on the magnitude of the earthquake, and the distance from the earthquake focus. At the epicentre of a powerful shallow quake, the shaking is so severe that even the strongest buildings may not survive.

Earthquakes also break apart the ground along faults. During an earthquake, the ground either side of a fault can shift sideways or up and down. The movement can be just a fraction of a centimetre or many metres. The massive Alaskan quake in 1964 shifted entire mountains upwards by 12 m (40 ft). When the shifting ground is in open country, the movement does little damage. In cities, it can snap in two anything from pipes, drains, and sewers, to buildings and bridges.

Sometimes, earthquakes set off landslides as they shake large soil banks, loose stones, or even solid slabs of rock down steep slopes. One of the most tragic examples happened in Peru in 1970 when an earthquake caused a rock avalanche that killed 18,000 people. When landslides are set off under the sea, they can generate **tsunami** waves.

The photo shows shifted ground created by the Landers earthquake that struck California, USA, in 1992. The quake measured 7.3 on the Richter scale.

## Kashmir 2005

On 8 October 2005, one of the worst earthquakes in recent years hit Kashmir in the mountains to the north of India and Pakistan (see photo below). The quake was set off by the gradual northward drift of the Indian plate into the giant plate that forms most of the rest of Asia. The quake was so powerful – 7.6 on the Richter scale – that the ground shifted 6.5 m (21 ft). Around 80,000 people died, entire villages were demolished, and 80 percent of the town of Uri was destroyed. Even recently erected schools collapsed, which led to criticisms over the quality of the building work. A total of 2.8 million people were left homeless. With the bitter mountain winter fast-approaching, only a massive international relief effort prevented an even greater tragedy.

## THE SCIENCE YOU LEARN: FAULTS

Faults are cracks in the rock where one big block of rock has slipped past another. Sometimes the moving block may be no bigger than a house. Sometimes it can be an entire mountain range. The block may move in a slow, continuous creep, or it can move with a sudden, large jump. Geologists classify faults according to how the rock moves. In a dip-slip fault, one block of rock slips down. In a reverse, or thrust, fault, one block is pushed up over the other. In strike-slip faults, the blocks move sideways past each other.

# Turning solid ground to liquid

When earthquakes hit ground made of loose sand and silt, they can actually turn the ground to liquid. This process is called **liquefaction**.

Normally, loose sands and soils are partly stuck together by moisture between the grains. When an earthquake's shear (S) waves move through them, the sand's grain structure is broken up. The water in the spaces between the grains pushes the grains apart. As a result, the sand briefly turns to a sticky liquid, like quicksand. The ground starts to flow, and anything heavy on the surface, such as buildings, roads, and bridges, may sink. The result can be devastating.

In many earthquakes, the worst hit areas are those built on loose sands and silts, such as in the Niigata quake in Japan in 1964.

## 🧠 THE SCIENCE YOU LEARN: SURFACE TENSION

Soil and loose sand often stay damp even when it's not raining. This is because surface tension stops the water draining away. Surface tension is the force that makes water drops spherical (round). Molecules in water attract each other. In the middle of a drop, the molecules pull equally in all directions. At the surface, molecules are only pulled inwards, since there are no molecules to pull outwards. The water makes its surface as small as possible, forming a ball. Surface tension also keeps water clinging to grains of soil and sand, and helps bind the grains together. Liquefaction happens when the shaking of an earthquake overcomes the surface tension binding the grains together.

## The 1989 Loma Prieta earthquake

On 18 October 1989, the San Andreas fault in California, USA shifted. The Loma Prieta quake, as it came to be called, was the most powerful in the region for almost a century. It rated 6.9 on the Richter scale. More than 60 people died, almost 4,000 were injured, and more than 12,000 were left homeless. The worst damage was in areas built on loose, wet soils and sands, such as the Marina district and the Monterey Bay shoreline north of San Francisco. The ground in these areas quickly liquefied, causing many buildings to collapse.

The Loma Prieta earthquake caused the collapse of a section of the Cypress Street Viaduct in Oakland, California, killing 42 people.

**Harbor Terminals SECOND RIGHT**

## CUTTING EDGE: EARTHSHAKING

The earthquake that hit Sumatra on 26 December 2004 and caused the Asian tsunami (see page 41) was the most powerful earthquake the world had seen for 40 years. It moved entire islands and may have actually made the whole Earth wobble. French earthquake scientist Paul Tarponnier, said it was like "flicking a top". The quake gave the Earth such a jolt that it actually shifted on its axis. It only shifted by about 2.5 cm (1 inch), but it was enough to tilt the Earth slightly towards the Sun and make all our days 2.7-millionths of a second longer.

## Earthquake damage

Although earthquakes are powerful, natural events, they actually kill few people directly. When the biggest earthquake ever recorded hit Chile in 1960, only 2,000 people were killed. The shaking of the ground rarely kills people. It may make them slip and break a limb, or fall into a crack in the ground. Yet many big earthquakes do very little damage. In fact, every year there is at least one magnitude 8.0 earthquake that takes few lives.

It is usually the collapse of man-made structures that turns a quake into a killer. When a big earthquake hits a city, people are crushed inside falling buildings or by collapsing bridges. When a dam breaks, it can unleash a devastating surge of water. In many quakes, the worst danger comes from fires that start when buildings collapse or underground gas pipes break. In the Great Kanto Earthquake of 1923, fires that were started by overturned cooking stoves engulfed the city of Tokyo in Japan.

Occasionally, earthquakes can wreak havoc naturally by setting off a landslide or triggering a deadly tsunami wave (see page 40). However, it is mostly the effect on man-made structures that is so damaging. This is why many people believe that although we can't prevent earthquakes, we can limit the harm they do.

The people of San Francisco, USA, watch as their city burns after an earthquake in 1906.

This bridge in Turkey collapsed like a pack of cards in the great Izmit earthquake of 1999.

## The Kobe earthquake 1995

CASE STUDY

The Great Hanshin quake struck the city of Kobe on 16 January 1995. It was the worst earthquake to hit Japan in recent times. It wasn't the biggest quake, but its focus was only 20 km (12 miles) away from Kobe and 16 km (10 miles) beneath nearby Awaji Island. It rated 7.5 on the Ms scale and 6.8 on the Mw scale. More than 6,000 people were killed and 26,000 injured.

In the port and wharf area of the city, liquefaction caused widespread collapse of warehouses, cranes, and docking facilities. The spectacular collapse of the Hanshin elevated expressway featured on the front page of newspapers around the world. The Japanese construct major buildings to withstand quakes, so most city centre buildings survived. The fatalities were mainly in the suburbs, where broken gas mains set fire to old wooden houses. Many traditional houses are lightly built, but have heavy tiled roofs to withstand typhoon winds. When the earthquake struck, the heavy roofs made the flimsy houses collapse like pancakes. Since the quake, homes have been rebuilt with stronger walls and lighter roofs. The *Guinness Book of Records* rates the Kobe quake as the most expensive natural disaster ever, causing more than U.S. $200 billion worth of damage.

# Earthquake prediction

Scientists now know that earthquakes occur when faults suddenly rupture. The problem is to work out just when it's going to happen, or to make any long-term prediction. One approach is to look at the record of past quakes. This technique is called **palaeoseismology**. Essentially, if you live in an earthquake zone where there has not been an earthquake for some time, you should expect one soon. The longer it has been since a quake, the bigger the quake will be. This is because there has been plenty of time for the strain in the rocks to build up.

In the past, scientists expected earthquakes to happen in **seismic gaps**. These are sections of faults where no earthquakes have occurred for some time. The scientists reasoned that tension must surely be building up in these places, and that they must snap soon. Yet when faults around the Pacific Ocean were monitored in the 1980s, it was discovered that earthquakes occurred slightly less in seismic gaps.

Russian seismologist Vladimir Keilis-Borok and his team devised a computer quake prediction model. It was based on the idea that chains of small quakes, or **foreshocks**, might happen before a big quake. Keilis-Borok calls the idea "the tail wags the dog" model. Using this model, the team successfully forecast big quakes almost a year in advance in both California and Japan in 2003. But a quake they predicted for southern California in 2004 never happened. The method has a long way to go. Many earthquakes do not seem to be preceded by any kind of foreshock.

Fault    City

Epicentres:
- magnitude 3.0 or lower
- magnitude 3.0-4.0
- magnitude 4.0-5.0

This diagram of a fault shows the sites where earthquakes have occurred over several decades. The central part, where the city is built, has not ruptured lately. This means that the risk of an earthquake there in the near future is high.

## The Turkish earthquake of 1999

On 17 August 1999, a magnitude 7.4 earthquake struck Izmit in Turkey, killing more than 15,000 people. However, the tragedy may have revealed data that will help predict earthquakes. Earthquakes may occur in clusters. One quake sets up stress further along a fault. The stress is then released in another quake.

American scientist Ross S Stein believes this is happening in Turkey. The Izmit earthquake was set off by movement along part of the North Anatolian fault, which stretches 1,400 km (875 miles) right across northern Turkey (see the map below). Since 1939, there has been a series of earthquakes along the fault, each one a little further west.

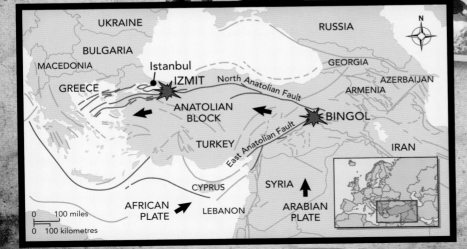

## Watching the ground

Earthquake scientists are not optimistic about ever predicting earthquakes long before they happen, but they might be able to find signs that indicate a quake is on its way. It would then be possible to warn people in time so they could prepare.

Many seismologists believe the answer is to watch for signs of strain building up in the rocks. In many earthquake zones, surveys now monitor the rocks in the ground for signs of deformation (shape change). Accurate surveys carried out on the surface may pick up slight horizontal movements, while tiltmeters set underground may pick up vertical movements.

Space satellites are the most exciting tools in earthquake prediction. Satellites can continuously scan wide areas of the Earth's surface for tiny changes in the land surface. Satellite laser ranging (SLR) can reveal the sideways movement of a tectonic plate by just a fraction of a centimetre. To make these measurements, laser beams are shone from the ground into space where they are reflected by the satellites.

In the future, another satellite system called InSAR may even spot slight variations in the height of the ground. The satellite takes pairs of radar images with two cameras a small way apart. From small differences in the pairs revealed by computer, InSAR may detect a change in ground height of less than 1 mm (0.04 in). Scientists are now trying to set up a network of InSAR satellites called the Global Earthquake Satellite System (GESS) to continuously monitor earthquake zones around the world.

Engineers in France work on the *Demeter* satellite shortly before its launch in 2004.

In the meantime, Global Positioning System (GPS) satellites may help. GPS satellites may not pick up vertical movements, but they can reveal slight horizontal movements almost instantly. In the 15 minutes before the 2004 Sumatra quake started, GPS satellites showed that the ground in Medan, Indonesia surged 14 cm (5.5 in) westwards. All of this remains speculation. Even when scientists do detect slight shifts and movement in the ground, there is still no way of knowing if and when an actual quake will begin.

The shadow in the water is a large plankton bloom in the Atlantic Ocean off the coast of Africa. It was photographed from the space shuttle *Discovery*.

## CUTTING EDGE: SATELLITE POWER

Detecting ground movement is not the only way in which satellites can be useful in predicting earthquakes. Satellites can also detect infrared (IR) radiation, which shows the heat of the ground. Just before a quake in Gujarat, India in 2001, NASA's Terra satellite detected an increase in IR radiation. It showed a slight warming of the ground. Another idea is to monitor the ocean for subtle changes in colour that reveal blooms (massive growths) of tiny sea organisms called plankton. Dr Ramesh Singh of Kanpur, India, thinks plankton blooms occur prior to earthquakes because the coming quake releases heat into the ocean. "If the epicentre of a quake lies very close to the coast," Dr Singh says, "then the [bloom is] clearly visible along that coast."

## Earthquake warnings

In their search for ways to predict earthquakes, seismologists are hunting for precursors – advance signs that an earthquake could be on its way. Some scientists believe that a rise in the water level in wells and boreholes indicates that an earthquake is coming. They say that stress in the rock squeezes the water in it up towards the surface. Another sign could be traces of radon gas squeezed out of the rocks in the same way.

Three Greek scientists have developed an earthquake prediction method that detects disturbances in natural electric currents flowing in the ground. By using this system, Japanese seismologists detected strange electromagnetic signals two months before a major earthquake. However, many scientists still question this method.

It has also long been believed that animals are sensitive to impending earthquakes. Dogs are said to howl, pandas moan, and fish thrash about in ponds. Some scientists are studying animals to see if they are picking up on indicators that could help predict earthquakes.

People often report seeing strange lights in the sky just before an earthquake. Scientists believe these **earthquake lights** could be caused by electrical changes in the ground. The photo shows lights in the sky at Mount Kimyo just before the 1966 earthquake in Matsushiro, Japan.

## Chinese quakes

China has experienced some terrible earthquakes, including the 1976 Tangshan tragedy in which up to 750,000 died. But Chinese quakes may provide clues in the hunt for earthquake warnings. In the day before the 1974 Haicheng quake, strange animal behaviour and a slight increase in ground tremors was enough to persuade authorities to evacuate the city. In the days before the Sichuan quake of 2008, which killed more than 60,000 people, thousands of frogs were seen in the streets. Satellites also detected strong electrical disturbances in the upper atmosphere. Some NASA scientists believe these are triggered by electrical changes in the ground as tectonic plates shift – possibly the best warning signals of a quake yet discovered.

N

**CHINA**

Shenyang • Fushun

Anshan

Magnitude 7.3
4 February 1975

Haicheng

Beijing

Tangshan

**NORTH KOREA**

Tianjin

Dalian

Magnitude 7.8
28 July 1976

Korea Bay

Shijiazhuang

Bo Hai

YELLOW SEA

CHINA

0   100 miles
0   100 kilometres

Qingdao

This photo shows the devastation caused in Tangshan by a massive earthquake in 1976.

# Preparing for earthquakes

Once scientists have identified earthquake hot spots, they can start to make hazard maps. These show areas where quakes are most likely to strike, and indicate to people living in these areas that they should be prepared.

In some high-risk areas there are education programmes to teach people how to prepare for an earthquake. In Japan, children learn earthquake safety drills from an early age. Japanese schoolchildren are taught to put on padded hats and duck under desks whenever the earthquake alarm goes off. This is to avoid being hit by falling objects such as ceiling tiles. Teachers also learn earthquake drills. For instance, it is important to close curtains to avoid flying glass, and to open doors so that they don't get jammed shut during the quake, trapping the children.

Every September, on the anniversary of the Great Kanto quake that hit Tokyo in 1923, 800,000 people take part in a full-scale earthquake drill. In the drill, the Japanese prime minister broadcasts the news of a bad earthquake to the nation and police. Firefighters and volunteers practise their emergency response.

The "Virtual California" computer simulator uses records of past earthquakes to calculate the probability of future quakes in California, USA. The simulation data indicates a 25 percent chance of a magnitude 7.0 earthquake in the San Francisco area in the next 20 years. In this computer graphic, the colour bars represent earth movement around the San Andreas fault.

## Mexico City 1985

On 19 September 1985, a magnitude 8.0 earthquake struck Mexico. There was widespread damage across the country, but particularly in the capital Mexico City. Here, more than 400 buildings collapsed and more than 3,000 were severely damaged. The worst affected area was a former lake bed where the loose sediments liquefied during the quake. Surprisingly, most of the tallest and shortest buildings – those with more than 20 storeys and fewer than 5 storeys – survived in the worst hit area. More than 70 percent of buildings with between 10 and 20 stories were wrecked. It turned out that the medium-height buildings swayed in time with the ground as it moved to and fro. Taller buildings swayed too slowly and shorter buildings too fast. Today, medium-height buildings are no longer built in Mexico City.

Istanbul in Turkey could be in as much danger as Mexico City. This huge city lies on the western end of the Anatolian fault, not far from the site of the great Izmit earthquake in 1999. Scientists fear that the city may soon be hit by a big earthquake.

## CUTTING EDGE: SOUNDING OUT THE CENTRE

Crucial rescue time is often lost after a quake strikes because the emergency services do not know exactly where to send the majority of the paramedics, bulldozers, and supplies. Even in big cities it is hard to assess the extent of the damage accurately on the ground. Communication can also be disrupted by a quake.

By traditional methods, it can take days for seismologists to work out just how big an earthquake is, and the location of its focus. Now, U.S. scientists are developing a system that uses ultrasound (sound too high-pitched for the human ear to hear) to analyse the location. With this system, they can pinpoint the epicentre of a quake within half an hour.

# Earthquake proofing

When a big quake strikes, most of the damage involves buildings and other city structures. Some cities and buildings survive a bad earthquake much better than others, simply because they are better built to withstand the shaking.

Surprisingly, skyscrapers are more likely to survive than short office blocks or homes. An earthquake makes a building sway. The taller it is, the more easily it sways. Shorter buildings are stiffer, and so get more jolted when the ground shakes. This effect can be felt by standing on a crowded bus or train. People are jolted much more if they stand rigidly than if they relax and sway with the movement of the vehicle.

## CUTTING EDGE: EARTHQUAKE SIMULATION

No matter how strong a building is in theory, the only way architects can be sure their buildings will stand a quake is to shake it and see. Some buildings in Los Angeles, USA, and Kobe, Japan, were constructed to the highest standards, yet still fell down when a quake hit. Now, architects are trying out their designs on **shake tables**. These platforms are shaken by motors to exactly simulate an earthquake. The earliest shake tables were only big enough to try out small models. Today, tables are being built to shake-test full-scale buildings.

At the 2005 U.N. World Conference on Disaster Reduction in Kobe, Japan, conference members watch a "shake table" test between a normal model building (destroyed) and a quake-resistant model building.

The Transamerica Pyramid in San Francisco, California, USA, has a 16-metre (52-foot) deep steel and concrete foundation, which is designed to move with earthquakes. The building successfully withstood the Loma Prieta earthquake of 1989.

Skyscrapers in quake zones should be designed so that the energy of the seismic waves is passed easily through the full height of the building – then back down again. For this to happen, floors and walls must bend a little. Often, the impact of the shaking is less if the building is mounted on base isolators, which allow the ground to move a little without the building moving. These may be dampers – rubberized or steel cushions that squeeze a little as the ground moves up beneath the building, and stretch as it goes down. Or they can be lubricated plates. These plates slide easily beneath the building as the ground moves sideways. Sometimes, tall buildings have a large tank of water in the upper floors called a slosh tank. The water in the tank absorbs some of the earthquake's energy as it sloshes back and forth.

The most important thing, though, is to strengthen buildings. Buildings are most affected by sideways movement. They will collapse if the walls sway in and out too much. A truss is a strengthening bar that runs between walls to hold them together. Even small houses survive earthquakes much better if the walls have trusses. Big buildings have elaborate networks of diagonal trusses that strengthen them against both horizontal and vertical shaking.

## Preparing for a quake

You can increase your chances of surviving an earthquake by being prepared. First of all, you must recognize when a quake is coming. The first sign is often a loud bang or roar. Then the ground may shake violently, and pitch and roll like a ship for several seconds or even minutes. Over the next few hours or days, aftershocks (smaller quakes) may follow.

There is no time to work out what to do on the spot. It is important that you have a plan beforehand, and go over it again and again until it is automatic. The key thing to remember when a quake strikes is to be protected from falling objects. Safety organizations tell people to remember to "Drop, Cover, Hold". This means that you should drop to the ground, cover your head, and hold on to a safe place until the motion has stopped.

Schoolchildren in Tokyo, Japan hide under their desks as part of a nationwide earthquake drill.

### ARE YOU IN AN EARTHQUAKE HOTSPOT?

No scientist can guarantee an area is safe from earthquakes. However, certain places are less likely to be hit. The Global Seismic Hazard Assessment Program produces maps that show how likely everywhere in the world is to suffer a quake. You can see them at www.seismo.ethz.ch/GSHAP/.

## When a quake strikes

- When indoors, duck under a desk or strong table. Stay away from shelves, cabinets, top-heavy furniture, mirrors, hanging plants, and anything that could fall. Beware of falling plaster or ceiling tiles. Stay in the "safe" place until all the motion has stopped.
- In a tall building, get under a desk or stand near an interior wall, but avoid staircases and lifts.
- In a crowded shop, stay there but move away from display shelves where things could fall.
- In a stadium or theatre, people should duck and protect their heads with their arms, a bag, or a coat. No-one should rush for the exit.
- If outdoors, stand well-clear of trees, signs, buildings, or electrical wires.
- If on a narrow street, duck into a doorway for protection from falling bricks.
- If in a car, pull over, but avoid overpasses, bridges, and power lines.
- If in a wheelchair, you should lock the wheels, and protect your head with your arms.

## When the shaking stops

- Be prepared for aftershocks.
- Open cabinets cautiously. Beware of objects that can fall off shelves.
- Stay away from damaged areas unless assistance has been specifically requested by police, fire, or relief organizations.
- Check for injuries. Give first aid as necessary.
- Remain calm and reassure others.
- Avoid broken glass.
- Check for fire. Take appropriate actions and precautions.
- Check gas, water, and electric lines. If damaged, shut off service. If gas is leaking, do not use matches, torches, appliances, or electric switches. Open windows, leave the building, and report the problem to a gas company.
- Replace all telephone receivers and use for emergency calls only.
- Tune to the emergency broadcast station on the radio or television. Listen for emergency bulletins.
- Stay out of damaged buildings.

# Tsunami

A tsunami is a wave that can be far bigger than any storm wave. The name is Japanese and means "harbour wave". Tsunamis got their name because every now and then Japanese fisherman would come home to find their village devastated by a wave that seemed to have risen up out of nothing in the harbour. This is partly true. Tsunamis travel from their origin, along the seabed, and only rear up to their full height when they reach shallow waters. They can pass right beneath a boat without even being noticed.

Tsunamis are essentially giant slops – rather like the water that slops over the sides of a small swimming pool if you do a bellyflop into it. The only difference is that tsunamis are not started by a mass landing on the surface. Instead they are started underwater by movement on the seabed. A few are generated by seabed landslides or volcanic eruptions, but most begin when a seabed fault moves during an earthquake. The sudden movement sets water travelling along the seabed away from the quake at astonishing speeds.

The diagram shows how a tsunami can be triggered when the earth below the sea either drops downwards or pushes upwards relative to the sea level.

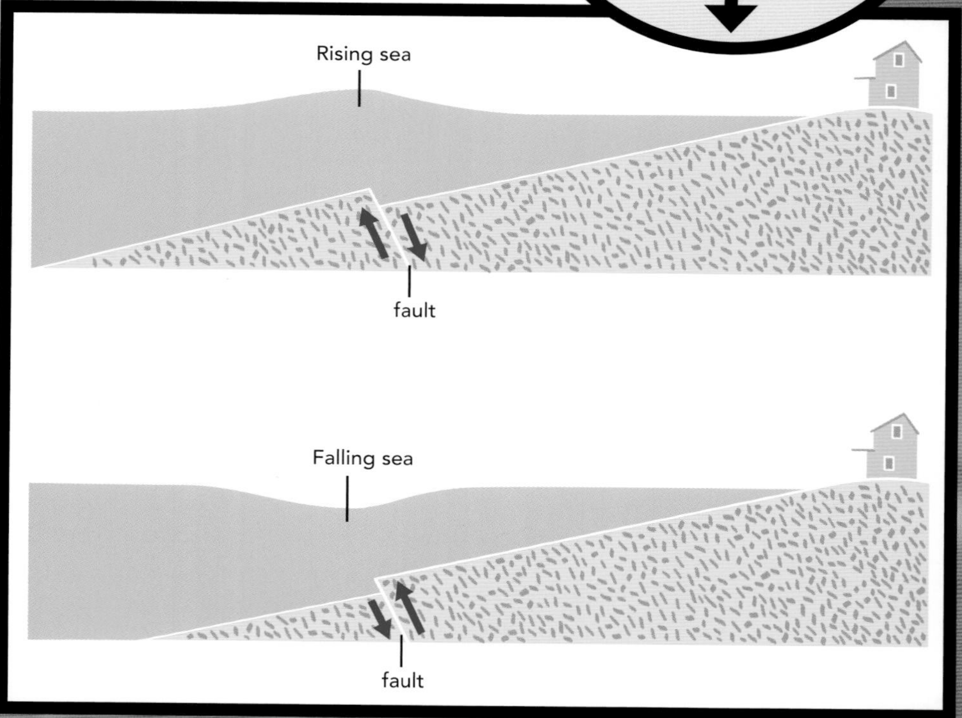

Rising sea

fault

Falling sea

fault

## The Boxing Day Tsunami

On 26 December 2004, the seabed off the coast of Sumatra in Southeast Asia was rocked by the second biggest earthquake ever recorded. It had a magnitude of 9.3 and lasted a massive eight minutes. The earthquake ripped apart the seabed and lifted it 20 m (66 ft) along a huge stretch of fault. This sudden upthrust moved billions of cubic metres of water and unleashed a devastating tsunami which claimed the lives of 230,000 people.

On the shores directly facing the quake, the tsunami reared up more than 30 m (98 ft) and reached more than 1.6 km (1 mile) on to the land. The Sumatran city of Banda Aceh was hit by the full force of the tsunami and was destroyed almost completely, killing tens of thousands of people. Within half an hour, the tsunami had swamped the Andaman Islands hundreds of kilometres away. Within one and a half hours it had overwhelmed the coastal resorts of Thailand with a wall of water 10 metres (33 ft) high. Within two hours, the tsunami hit Sri Lanka and India. Even 8,500 km (5,280 miles) away in South Africa, a 1.5 metres (5 ft) high wave surged on the shore, 16 hours after the quake. Lessons have been learned from this disaster, and now there are plans to set up a tsunami warning system (see page 44) in the Indian Ocean.

Identification of locations to be warned based on model outputs

Following the devastating 2004 tsunami, the Indian government opened a National Early Warning System for Tsunami and Storm Surges in the Indian Ocean. The centre can issue alerts of killer waves within 13 minutes of an earthquake. Scientists are working to reduce this time by half.

# Tsunami strike

Sometimes tsunamis are called **tidal waves** because the sea seems to rise smoothly like a tide, rather than breaking like a storm wave. However, tsunamis are nothing to do with tides, and there is usually more than one of them. There were three big waves in the tsunami on 26 December 2004, and a series of smaller ones that continued for hours afterwards.

Out at sea, tsunamis are almost invisible on the surface because they travel along the seabed. They move at incredible speeds, often 700 kph (435 mph) or more, which is faster than a jet airliner. The deeper the water, the smaller the wave on the surface and the faster it travels. At such speeds, they can travel right across the widest ocean in a matter of hours. Because they are travelling so fast, there can be up to 100 km (62 miles) between each small wave crest. This is why they can pass unnoticed by ships in the ocean.

Once they reach shallow water, tsunamis suddenly become all too noticeable. They may slow down a little, but like water slopping up the edge of a bath, they can rear up to frightening heights. The crest or the trough of the wave can hit land first. If the trough hits first, the sea recedes like a tide suddenly going out. In the tsunami on 26 December 2004, a kilometre or more of beach was suddenly exposed in some places. Many people ventured out to collect stranded fish – with terrible consequences when the wave crest rolled in minutes later. In Phuket, Thailand, 10-year-old British tourist Tilly Smith remembered this about tsunamis from a geography lesson at school. She warned her parents and others on the beach to run inland in time to save their lives.

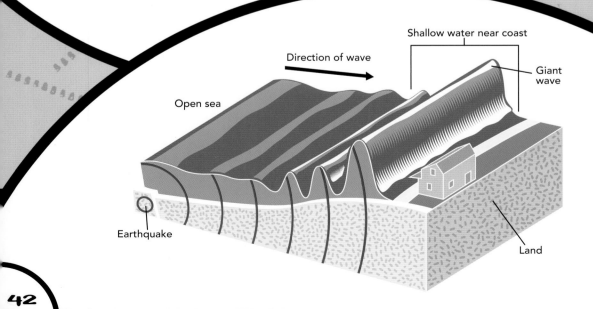

Shallow water near coast

Direction of wave

Open sea

Giant wave

Earthquake

Land

A terrifying wall of water hits the shoreline in Thailand during the 2004 tsunami disaster.

## The Eltanin meteor impact tsunami

Not all tsunamis are set off by earthquakes. Tsunamis can be started by the impact of a meteor from space, like a giant stone thrown in a pond. Although rare, impact tsunamis can be gigantic. Geologists have found evidence that 2.2 million years ago, the Earth was hit by a meteor landing in the Pacific Ocean 1,500 km (930 miles) west of Chile. There are signs of a massive crater on the seabed, called the Eltanin crater. When the meteor hit the water, it sent out a tsunami more than 300 m (985 ft) high all around the Pacific Ocean. Remains of fish have been found washed far inland in both Chile and Antarctica by this massive wave. Impact tsunamis like these probably occur every couple of million years, and there have probably been many bigger ones in the course of the Earth's history.

# Tsunami warning and defences

Unlike earthquakes, tsunamis can take a little while to arrive if you are some distance from the epicentre. This means there could be time to issue a warning before it strikes.

In the Pacific Ocean, the first tsunami warning system was set up in 1946 after a tsunami hit the Hawaiian town of Hilo. Nowadays, the Pacific Tsunami Warning System goes on alert every time the Global Seismographic Network (see page 17) detects a large, shallow quake under the sea. Before a warning is issued, evidence is needed that a tsunami is actually running across the ocean floor. Dotted across the ocean floor are pressure sensors that form the DART (Deep Ocean Assessment and Reporting of Tsunamis) system. DART's ocean floor sensors detect slight changes in water pressure. The changes in pressure are caused by a rise or fall in the depth of the water above by as little as 1 mm (0.04 in). Each sensor is linked to a buoy on the surface. If there is a sudden change in water depth, the bouy sends out the alarm via a satellite link. DART readings are combined with readings from tide gauges measuring water depth on the coast.

## CUTTING EDGE: JAPANESE TSUNAMI WARNING

No country is more alert to the dangers of tsunamis than Japan. The Japanese have the most sophisticated tsunami warning system in the world. An elaborate network of more than 300 sensors on the islands and in the sea constantly monitor any slight change in ocean depth. Seismographs continually check on quake activity. If a quake looks like it might cause a tsunami, the Japanese Meteorological Association (JMA) can issue an alert in just three minutes. The system is so refined that it can predict the height, speed, destination, and arrival time of any tsunami. In the past, the alert went out just on radio and television channels. In recent years, alerts have been sent out by text message to everyone with a mobile phone in the danger area.

In September 2007, a similar system worked in Sri Lanka when the Sri Lankan Disaster Management Centre sent out text messages to warn people about an approaching tsunami. The message read, "Tsunami warning for Sri Lanka north, east and south coast. People asked to move away from coast – Disaster Management Centre."

Early warnings may help people to evacuate coastal areas before a tsunami strikes. The impact of tsunamis can also be reduced by barriers on the shore. The Japanese have built seawalls several metres high along the coast to protect against tsunamis. The United Nations Environment Program (UNEP) also found that the damage caused by the 26 December tsunami was less severe where the shoreline was protected by coral reefs or by vegetation, especially mangrove swamps. Unfortunately, these natural defences are at risk from pollution, deforestation, tourism, and excessive fish farming.

A simulated tsunami wave of 2.5-metres high swallows a model wooden house at a tsunami simulator facility at the Port and Airport Research Institute in Yokosuka, Japan.

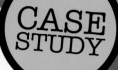

## Mega-tsunami

Back in 1958, two geologists searching for oil in Alaska witnessed an awesome sight. A cliff collapsed into a bay and sent out a wave more than 0.5 km (0.3 miles) high – higher than most skyscrapers. Fortunately, this wave was confined to an Alaskan bay. Scientists began to wonder what effect a really big landslide would have. They began to talk about mega-tsunamis and look for evidence of giant waves in the past. They found that the biggest danger comes from volcanic islands. When the side of a volcanic island collapses during an eruption, it can dump half a mountain into the sea. This would create a colossal wave.

It was then that scientists noticed the side of the volcano Cumbre Vieja on La Palma in the Canary Islands. The volcano is quiet at the moment, but scientists believe it could rumble back into life at any time. There is a giant block of the mountainside, which weighs around 5 billion tonnes (5.5 billion tons), poised ready to slip into the Atlantic Ocean. If it does slip, it could create a tsunami 600 metres (1,970 ft) high, which would rush across the Atlantic at the speed of a jet plane. By the time it hit the eastern United States a few hours later, it would be about 50 metres (165 ft) high. The huge wave would sweep away everything in its path up to 20 km (12 miles) inland. It would hit Boston first, then New York, and all the coastal cities down to Miami. The wave would look something like the one in the 2004 disaster film *The Day After Tomorrow*.

The people of New York City, USA, flee from an onrushing tidal wave on the set of the film, *The Day After Tomorrow*. →

## What progress have we made?

Approximately half the world's major cities are located in earthquake zones. Hundreds of millions of people go about their daily lives with the threat of a major quake. The number of vulnerable people grows each day because earthquake-prone cities like Mexico City, Shanghai, and Tokyo are expanding rapidly. Seismologists are certain that sooner or later, one of these cities will be hit by a major quake.

Over the last 50 years, seismologists have made great progress in understanding how earthquakes begin, and why they occur in certain areas. They have also built up a sophisticated network of monitoring equipment, which allows them to keep a constant check on the Earth and its movements. They can tell when an earthquake begins anywhere in the world, and they can detect the movement of the Earth's surface by just a fraction of a centimetre. Yet despite all this, they are not much nearer being able to predict just when and how powerfully an earthquake will strike.

# Facts and figures

## Deadliest earthquakes on record

---

**DATE:** 23 January 1556
**LOCATION:** Shansi, China
**DEATHS:** 830,000
**STRENGTH:** 8.0
**EFFECTS:** This was the worst earthquake in history and killed more than 800,000 people. Many people lived in artificial caves called yaodang. These were cut in soft rock and collapsed catastrophically when the quake hit. According to Chinese records, "Mountains and rivers changed places and roads were destroyed. In some places, the ground suddenly rose up and formed new hills, or it sank abruptly and became new valleys. In other areas, a stream burst out in an instant, or the ground broke and new gullies appeared. Huts, official houses, temples, and city walls collapsed suddenly."

---

**DATE:** 27 July 1976
**LOCATION:** Tangshan, China
**DEATHS:** 255,000 (estimated)
**STRENGTH:** 7.5
**EFFECTS:** This was the worst earthquake disaster of the 20th century, and the second worst ever. Some estimates suggest nearly 750,000 were killed and another 799,000 were injured. Damage reached as far as Beijing, hundreds of kilometres away.

---

**DATE:** 9 August 1138
**LOCATION:** Aleppo, Syria
**DEATHS:** 230,000
**STRENGTH:** Not known
**EFFECTS:** In the 12th century, Syria was ravaged by wars between the Christian Crusaders and the Muslim Saracens. Aleppo was a large Crusader city. Although the city was virtually destroyed, most of the inhabitants had been warned by foreshocks and escaped to the countryside. Most of the deaths were in the villages of nearby Antioch in southern Turkey.

---

**DATE:** 26 December 2004
**LOCATION:** West coast of northern Sumatra
**DEATHS:** More than 225,000
**STRENGTH:** 9.0
**EFFECTS:** This was one of the largest quakes in the last 100 years. It was not the quake that did the damage, because it was on the seabed. Instead, the tsunami it generated spread around the Indian Ocean, hitting 14 different countries. It was the Earth's most deadly tsunami.

---

**DATE:** 22 December 1856
**LOCATION:** Damghan, Iran
**DEATHS:** 200,000
**STRENGTH:** Not known
**EFFECTS:** Damghan is one of the world's oldest cities. The earthquake destroyed many of its greatest buildings, as well as killing more than 200,000 people. This devastating earthquake was characterized by the large fractures that opened in the ground, as well as the terrible death toll.

**DATE:** 16 December 1920
**LOCATION:** Gansu, China
**DEATHS:** 200,000
**STRENGTH:** 7.8
**EFFECTS:** This giant earthquake was felt right across China. It did its damage not simply by bringing down buildings, but by setting off countless landslides, blocking rivers and changing their course, causing extensive flooding.

**DATE:** 23 March 1893
**LOCATION:** Ardabil, Iran
**DEATHS:** 150,000
**STRENGTH:** Not known

**DATE:** 1 September 1923
**LOCATION:** Kanto, Tokyo, Japan
**DEATHS:** 143,000
**STRENGTH:** 7.9
**EFFECTS:** The city of Tokyo was almost completely destroyed by the firestorm that swept through it after the quake, burning 381,000 houses. Altogether, 694,000 homes were destroyed.

**DATE:** 5 October 1948
**LOCATION:** Ashgabat, Turkmenistan
**DEATHS:** 110,000
**STRENGTH:** 7.3
**EFFECTS:** Almost all brick buildings were destroyed in the town of Ashgabat. Bridges collapsed and many freight trains were derailed.

**DATE:** 28 December 1908
**LOCATION:** Messina, Italy
**DEATHS:** 70,000–100,000 (estimated)
**STRENGTH:** 7.2
**EFFECTS:** More than 90 percent of buildings were destroyed in the ancient city of Messina in Sicily, and a tsunami caused devastation.

**DATE:** September 1290
**LOCATION:** Chihli, China
**DEATHS:** 100,000
**STRENGTH:** Not known
**EFFECTS:** This earthquake was not only characterized by the high death toll, but by the huge masses of rock that shifted during the quake.

**DATE:** 8 October 2005
**LOCATION:** Pakistan
**DEATHS:** 80,361
**STRENGTH:** 7.6
**EFFECTS:** The mountain region of Pakistan was badly hit by this quake, which killed more than 80,000 people directly and left countless people homeless. Landslides blocked or destroyed mountain roads, cutting villages off from help for many days.

**DATE:** November 1667
**LOCATION:** Shemakha, Caucasus Mountains
**DEATHS:** 80,000
**STRENGTH:** Not known

DATE: 18 November 1727
LOCATION: Tabriz, Iran
DEATHS: 77,000
STRENGTH: Not known

DATE: 25 December 1932
LOCATION: Gansu, China
DEATHS: 70,000
STRENGTH: 7.6

DATE: 1 November 1755
LOCATION: Lisbon, Portugal
DEATHS: 70,000
STRENGTH: 8.7 (estimated)
This earthquake occurred on All Saints Day when many of Lisbon's 250,000 inhabitants were in church. Many were crushed as the stone churches collapsed. Others sought safety down on the river front but were swept away by a large tsunami set off by landslides.

DATE: 31 May 1970
LOCATION: Peru
DEATHS: 66,000
STRENGTH: 7.9

DATE: 30 May 1935
LOCATION: Quetta, Pakistan
DEATHS: 30,000–60,000
STRENGTH: 7.5

DATE: 11 January 1693
LOCATION: Sicily, Italy
DEATHS: 60,000
STRENGTH: Not known

DATE: 1268
LOCATION: Silicia, Asia Minor
DEATHS: 60,000
STRENGTH: Not known

DATE: 30 May 1935
LOCATION: Quetta, Pakistan
DEATHS: 30,000–60,000
STRENGTH: 7.5

DATE: 4 February 1783
LOCATION: Calabria, Italy
DEATHS: 50,000
STRENGTH: Not known

DATE: 20 June 1990
LOCATION: Iran
DEATHS: 40,000–50,000
STRENGTH: 7.7

*Source: National Earthquake Information Center, U.S. Geological Survey. Data compiled from several sources.*

# Some projects to do

1. *Earthquake prediction*
   Use the Internet and your library to investigate whether anyone has a consistent, successful way to predict earthquakes. If not, why were they not successful? Come up with your own idea for predicting earthquakes, and test it. Explain why it did or did not work.

2. *Earthquake myths*
   Examine earthquake myths and interview people about these myths to find out what they think. What would be the best way to get rid of myths? Is there a group of people who tend to believe myths more? Older people? Younger people? Other groups?

3. *Seismic waves*
   What types of seismic waves are there? What do they look like on a seismogram? What effects do different kinds of waves have on different kinds of buildings?

4. *World-wide earthquake hazards*
   Which areas around the world are most vulnerable to earthquakes and why? What are the major problems when dealing with earthquakes in different areas?

5. *Earthquake preparedness*
   Research the most effective ways to prepare for an earthquake. Test the effectiveness of different types of earthquake brackets and straps, etc. Determine the safest places to be inside the house, outside, in the car, etc. Prepare an earthquake plan for your family, class, school.

6. *Earthquake-proof buildings*
   Try to design a building that can withstand an earthquake. What works? What does not work? Why?

# Find out more

## Books

*Encyclopedia of Earthquakes and Volcanoes* (3rd edn.), David Ritchie and Alexander E. Gates (Checkmark Books, 2007)

*Be an Earthquake Scientist (Using Science)*, Suzy Gazlay (ticktock Media Ltd., 2008)

*Volcanoes and Earthquakes (DK Eyewitness Books)*, Susanna van Rose (DK Publishing, 2004)

*Shaky Ground: Earthquakes (Freestyle: Turbulent Planet)*, Mary Colson (Raintree, 2005)

## Websites

### Earthquakes

http://earthquakes.usgs.gov/learning/index.php
Find out about earthquakes at the U.S. Geological Survey's site.

http://neic.usgs.gov/neis/qed
Find out out where earthquakes have occurred in the last month.

www.exploratorium.edu/faultline/damage/index.html
Find out more about coping with the dangers of earthquakes.

### Tsunami

www.tsunami.noaa.gov
Find out a lot more about tsunamis at the National Oceanic and Atmospheric Administration's Tsunami Centre.

http://nctr.pmel.noaa.gov/animate.html
See fascinating scientific animations of tsunamis, and tsunami monitoring systems.

www.ngdc.noaa.gov/hazard/tsu_db.shtml
Find out about all the tsunamis that have happened in history from the Global Tsunami Database.

## Activities to try

- The power of shock waves
Use this simple demonstration to see how the power of a shock wave
decreases further away from the epicentre. Scatter some sand on an old
table and tap the edge of the table with a rubber hammer. The shock wave
will make the sand jump in the air. Now move the sand further away from
the edge of the table and tap the table with the hammer again, equally
hard. This time the sand will not jump as high.

- Make your own tsunami
http://mceer.buffalo.edu/infoservice/Education/makeTsunamiDirections.asp

- The Exploratorium has a selection of models and demonstrations to try.

- Demonstrate how P waves travel:
www.exploratorium.edu/faultline/activezone/slinky.html

- Demonstrate how liquefaction occurs:
www.exploratorium.edu/faultline/activezone/liquefaction.html

- Record seismic motion on a car ride:
www.exploratorium.edu/faultline/activezone/highway.html

## More projects to do

- Compare the location of volcanoes and earthquake zones, and note the
similarities. Find out how eruptions are predicted.

- Find out whether there have been any/many earthquakes where you live,
even if they were very small.

- Find out how charities/aid organizations respond to earthquakes.

- For a list of projects to try and increase your knowledge of earthquakes
go to:
http://earthquake.usgs.gov/learning/kids/sciencefair.php

# Glossary

**body waves**   earthquake waves that move deep underground

**compressional wave**   (see primary wave)

**continental drift**   the way the Earth's continents move slowly around the world over tens of millions of years

**crust**   layer of rock and soil that forms the surface of the Earth

**earthquake lights**   strange lights and lightning seen in the sky at the time of an earthquake

**earthquake zone**   region where earthquakes frequently happen

**epicentre**   point on the surface above where an earthquake begins

**fault creep**   slow movement of rock either side of a fault

**focus**   centre of an earthquake where shaking begins

**foreshock**   slight shaking of the ground before a big earthquake

**hypocentre**   point underground where an earthquake begins

**intensity**   size of an earthquake judged by its effects

**liquefaction**   the way loose sediments can become like a liquid during an earthquake

**Love waves**   secondary earthquake waves become Love waves when they reach the surface. Love waves shake from side to side.

**magnitude**   the size of the biggest waves in an earthquake

**mantle**   deep layer of warm semi-liquid rock beneath the Earth's crust

**Mercalli scale**   measurement that rates the intensity of an earthquake according to the damage it does

**moment magnitude**   version of Richter earthquake scale that rates earthquakes according to both the magnitude (size) of their waves and their power to move rock

**palaeoseismology**   study of earthquakes in the past

**plate boundary**   line along which tectonic plates meet

**primary waves (P waves)**   waves that travel fastest and arrive first in an earthquake. They travel by alternately squeezing and stretching (compressing) the ground.

**Rayleigh waves**   primary earthquake waves become Rayleigh waves when they reach the surface. They squeeze and stretch the ground.

**Richter scale**   measurement from 0 to over 9, first devised by Charles Richter for rating the magnitude of the waves during an earthquake

**secondary waves**   waves that travel slightly less fast and arrive second in an earthquake. They travel by alternately squeezing and stretching the ground.

**seismic gap**   region in an earthquake zone where quakes have not occurred for some time – so may happen soon

**seismic waves**   vibrations in the ground set off by an earthquake

**seismogram**   record of an earth tremor made by a seismograph

**seismograph**   device for measuring and recording earthquake waves

**seismologist**   scientist who studies earthquakes and earthquake waves

**shake table**   motorized table used for experiments that shakes to mimic the effects of an earthquake

**shear waves (S waves)**   earthquake waves that move from side to side with a tearing effect

**surface waves**   earthquake waves that travel through the ground surface

**tectonic plates**   giant slabs of rock that make up the Earth's surface and move very slowly all the time

**tidal wave**   misleading name for a tsunami

**tsunami**   giant wave that can be created by the sudden movement of the seabed, for example, during an earthquake

# Index